5 Skills of Master Salespeople

A GUIDE TO THE HEART OF SELLING:
A PRIMER FOR BEGINNERS, A RESOURCE FOR VETERANS

Research-based advice about what to do and say that can make the difference between losing a sale and creating a loyal, confident customer

By Michael D. Maginn

SINGULARITY GROUP, INC.

Other Books by the Author

Effective Teamwork, McGraw-Hill, 1994

Making Teams Work, McGraw-Hill, 2004

Managing In Times of Change, McGraw-Hill, 2007

ISBN: 978-0-578-02796-8

Singularity Group, Inc., Box 416, Hamilton, MA 01936

Masters of Their Craft

Sales people are the beautiful people in an organization, the people people, the extroverts, the Big Picture people, the people with nice suits and tasteful ties. They are the talkers, the joke people, the smilers into the telephone. They tend to stifle giggles at internal technical presentations and roll their eyes when formulas and equations go up on the screen. They are the ones who could tell mild jokes at the customer's expense to the customer's face and get away with it. They have an open-faced, disarming honesty about what is good and bad about a product, a certain off-hand but, at the same time, penetrating way of matching a customer's need with a solution.

They travel together within a company, a separate group that seems highly charged, partly a moving party of short attention span brats, partly a platoon of battered front line heroes who somehow bring back signed orders. They have a dark, tenacious side that won't let competition breathe, street-fighters who have a sense of the jugular. They have painfully learned to handle rejection.

They live to make calls.

This is all covered by a bit of charm and bluster, some faux pained expressions, some humor switching easily to deep sincerity. They aren't technical geniuses; they are professional salespeople. They practice asking questions, they polish presentations, they work on the nuances of handling different objections. They hone their skill. They have the right stuff to be successful.

They are Masters of their Craft.

The advice in this guide is about what they do and how they do it.

Why This Advice?

I'm sorry to say there are no silver bullets nor secret ingredients to becoming a master salesperson. I wish there were, but they don't exist. There are no flashy techniques nor razzle-dazzle verbal acrobatics and word plays which will consistently produce new business. There are no personality profiles, pre-call visualizations, no scripts, canned responses, memorized spiels, worksheets, nor tricks for getting past the receptionist which, at the end of the day, make a bit of difference between high performers and average salespeople. There are hundreds of books and seminars which teach a million different techniques, but ask anyone who has read one what difference it has made. Sure, most people can extract one, two or three ideas or a phrase that's appealing or sounds fresh. They might even use it and tell their colleagues what happened. But does that make them masters of the craft? Hardly.

For over 25 years, I have been fortunate to have worked with and study high performing salespeople in a wide range of businesses and different modes of selling and for a number of different purposes. I've also sold professional consulting services for my own company. What I have found, net-net, is that people who do well, consistently, regardless of the industry or product, understand that, at the heart of selling, is meeting customer needs. How to do that is condensed into a few basic ideas that describe the skills of a successful salesperson.

Whether you sell over the phone, over a counter or in an office or conference room or shop floor or even through the mail, how you implement these ideas contribute a great deal to closing business or not. Sales professionals know this, and they practice and improve their skill execution like a pitcher working on a slider or a golfer focusing on chip shots.

This short guide will attempt to explain, as clearly as possible, the underlying, fundamental ideas of the selling process. The first section describes what I call "The Heart of Selling," and presents the role of salesperson as problem solver. The second section presents the five ideas which are central to understanding how to sell. In the third section, there is a repertoire of skills that make selling work, organized by each of the selling ideas. However, understanding the job is not performing the job. To become a master salesperson, you need to apply these concepts and get some feedback. In the fourth section, there are some ideas for doing that, but that process is up to you.

Objection: It's Not Me

At this point, you might feel what you need to become better at selling should be more specific to your world. You say industrial selling is different from telesales is different from retail is different from selling pharmaceuticals and 767s. Sure, there are differences in what salespeople in these scenarios do, but what I find fascinating is what is common to all these. That's what this advice is all about.

There is an underlying thread of meeting customer needs in all selling.

If you can understand the central ideas for doing that, you can apply those concepts with whatever adjustments you need to make to your own situation.

Hang in there. Your job is to see what's useful to you and apply it. Some of this might not be just right for you, but look for the thread. You can follow it right to the heart of selling.

Section 1: The Heart of Selling

At the very core of the matter is the question "What is selling all about?" Let's take a close look at what happens when a sale is successful and when it is not. We should be able to surface the core concept that selling is a problem solving exchange between customers with needs and a salesperson with a wide array of ways to address those needs. When the salesperson does that right, the customer gains confidence in the sales process and certainty that his/her decisions are right.

Tellin' Ain't Sellin'

Customers talk to you, the salesperson, because they sense a need—something is happening that shouldn't be happening or something isn't happening that should be. Most of the time, customers think they know what that gap is. After all, this is a world of sophisticated customers.

If you show a customer how your product or service fills the gap which they tell you about—the problem they think they have—that is not selling. That is describing. Anyone can do that, even your competitors, and rest assured, they will when their turn comes.

The customer is then left to choose between descriptions of products or services he or she has gathered from different sales people which will address what they perceive is their problem. Many sales situations are set up that way even by very sophisticated customers. For example, the department manager who sends out a Request For Proposal with a written description of "the need" will get in return descriptions of solutions at different costs. In selling by description, the buyer's choice often boils down to a price decision. Unless you are the low cost vendor, it is very difficult to succeed as a "describer".

Why?

A salesperson who describes products is not any different than a catalogue. The customer may well have just looked at the printed descriptions—lists of features—and made a choice. The customer is limiting the salesperson's role in the buying process to being a source of information, a responder to the customer's inquiries. The customer is asking the questions which revolve around "What is your product like, what features does it have, and how much does it cost?" In this kind of sales world, a salesperson can be successful only if he or she says what the customer wants to hear.

What does a customer get out of that kind of sales process? Information, a sense of what the product is or how it might work. But there is a distance between the need and the solution; the customer feels it and expresses it as doubt, uncertainty. If the customer buys something after this kind of sales process, it will not be with the highest confidence.

Master Selling

Real, effective selling, on the other hand, puts the salesperson in a more active, inquisitive, interactive catalyst role. When that happens, the distance between the buyer and the seller shrinks and confidence grows.

At the heart of selling is the process of problem solving. Problem solving means finding and understanding the broad array of customer needs and then providing unique and valuable ways to address them, using all the special knowledge, industry experience and context that the salesperson has. When the salesperson brings to light additional needs through questioning, eventually clarifying the underlying problems to be solved, the stage is set for a creative solution. The salesperson applies expert product, technical, business and industry knowledge, and the recommendations fit. The salesperson not only brings the best answer to the table, he or she also helps the customer avoid wasting time and effort on a sub-optimal approach.

As a result, the customer now looks as this sales process as valuable; confidence is built and he or she is more certain that the decision to buy is right.

Two Examples of Selling Beyond The Given Need
Ski Shop

A retail customer who wants to buy skis he's read about in a magazine walks into a local ski shop. After some questions, the salesperson discovers the customer skis on moderate terrain three weekends a year when the slopes are generally icy. The salesperson knows the skis he wants are suitable for this type of skiing only 25-35 percent of the time, and they are premium priced. The salesperson recommends a different ski by the same manufacturer that better fits the customer's pattern of usage and budget. The customer leaves with new skis, a new understanding of what to look for when buying skis and a positive feeling about the sales experience, the salesperson and the store.

Corporate environment

A corporate manager is the member of a task force associated with implementing a new organizational team structure. The purpose of the new structure is to allow sales and service teams to get close to their customers, serving them as efficiently as possible.

Through its discussions, the task force has decided that each of the new teams needs training in "team building skills". The task force's feeling is that teams need to bond, built new relationships, and learn how to build consensus and manage conflict. Training vendors are brought in to describe how they would accomplish the task and submit a proposal.

One of the vendors asks the customer penetrating questions about this change, the business reasons for it and its impact on team members as well as customers. The customer is impressed by her questions. She gets permission to interview other members of the task as well prospective team members. What comes to the surface after several discussions are a host of complicated needs: The new team members are resisting the change, there is a fear that customers will react negatively, team leaders are not confident about how to proceed. And the task force is preoccupied with other matters; the "team building skills" approach seemed to them like a logical answer.

To the vendor's salesperson, who has seen many corporations grapple with change, the team building solution is premature. What the team members really need is an orientation to the change, an explanation of how it will benefit them, time to create solutions to predictable problems the change will create, and a plan for the team to move forward. Skill building can come later.

When the customer and the task force were presented with the idea, they immediately saw how the recommended approach would help get the teams started. If they had embarked on "team building" training, which they all thought was a logical need, they would have made a costly mistake.

Other Needs Beyond The Product

Let's examine the concept further. The basic idea is if you identify a wide array of customer needs, you can provide a solution that solves a wide array of problems. When you do that, the customer sees the value you are bringing to the table, and he or she senses you are helping, not just selling.

Here's an example; let's look at commodity products. Because these products are virtually the same, the salesperson has to find other than product needs to address.

Commodities are products that are virtually indistinguishable. Think about the challenge of selling chemicals, steel beams, computer parts or paper in bulk. The customer has certain expectations about the product—the quality of the chemical and its price, for instance. Competitors match feature to feature and often price makes the difference.

However, if a salesperson just described the product and the price, he or she would miss out on a whole other area of customer needs that go beyond the product.

For example, a customer is buying hard drives, almost a commodity item in the technology business. The customer is strictly interested in a volume discount as price is a major decision criteria. Through questioning, the salesperson discovers the customer also has a need to stage orders over the course of a year. When pressed, the customer states the problem is the company's pattern of orders received, hence, production runs are erratic, and management would love a way to reduce the cost of carrying inventory during lulls. The salesperson performs an analysis, providing the customer with economic order quantities to buy and when, based on the customer's business and buying patterns. As a result, the customer is able to stock hard drives on a just-in-time basis at the best price.

The customer's underlying need was not so much buying disk drives of a certain type, but, rather, how to buy them.

Perhaps that customer had problems around credit, delivery schedules, warehousing, or returns. Once recognized, the salesperson should be able to make a recommendation on how the problem can be resolved or minimized. The recommended, comprehensive solution goes well beyond the product, and it addresses real customer needs, allowing the customer to buy with confidence.

Future Problems

Let's go another step in building the concept: Find a wide array of needs, even those in the future, and figure out how to address them.

The salesperson who goes beyond the here and now and into the future will also find customer needs. If future customer needs can, in some way, be acted on now, the salesperson will have demonstrated not only unique value, but a sincere interest in the customer and the customer's business and the relationship in the future.

Imagine the owner of a conveyor belt manufacturing company is placing an order with a vendor's salesperson. The salesperson learns through a side comment that the owner is thinking of buying a new building. The salesperson knows that designing the layout of the manufacturing floor in the new building will be an important need. Apparently, the owner hasn't thought about that. A need which will soon vex the owner has been tagged by the salesperson who has widened his view of the customer's world and has helped the customer recognize a future need. The stage is set. The salesperson can recommend that the owner get advice from the vendor company's design experts. The salesperson also recommends two independent architects who can discuss design options. Clearly, the salesperson is solving problems the owner hasn't addressed yet but will definitely need to in order to proceed with his idea. While there are no dollars exchanged for this service, the owner's loyalty to the vendor is enhanced, and the stage is set for future selling opportunities.

Selling the Total Package of Benefits

Every customer has problems to be solved. The point is that the salesperson has to go beyond the product need and into the wider array of needs customers have in buying, in making the buying decision, in using the product effectively as well as in the future of the business.

To do that successfully, the salesperson has to see what he or she is selling in a different way. The salesperson's offering is not a product or service or even a family of products or service. Rather, the offering is the total package of benefits associated with doing business with the salesperson's company. This extended concept of the offering—including the deal itself, the efforts of the vendor to make the product work and the customer's business successful now and in the future—gives the salesperson more solutions to apply to customer problems. The more solutions the salesperson brings, the more value the customer feels. When the salesperson brings a lot of value, the total offering—the full package of solutions to the broader array of customer needs—

starts to outweigh price objections or price-only advantages that the competition may have.

What is the total package of benefits?

Consider what a salesperson brings to the table. Typically, in the eyes of the customer, it's a product or service. The cost of entry into the sales relationship is that a salesperson must know and be able to explain the features and benefits of the product or service and how they are different from the competition's. Presumably, a good salesperson should be able to relate these features and benefits directly to customer needs. But, as I've indicated, products and services are not the only things a salesperson brings in.

Because of their company knowledge, industry expertise and exposure to a wide range of customers, the salesperson also has ideas and information about payment terms, availability, delivery, installation, support and application concepts, and even credit and billing options.

For example, if a furniture salesperson purposely looks for and identifies delivery timing as a need of a two-job family who are home for short periods and at odd hours, and then sells a choice of delivery options, he or she is selling a wider view of the offering. And the customers get more than just a couch.

A salesperson also brings ideas about customization, about how the basic product can be modified or configured for a specific customer use. Customization may be related to the actual product itself, the financial relationship or any other aspect of doing business with the vendor company. When the salesperson searches for and finds a felt need for adapting the product to make it fit more effectively, then he or she can explain how the vendor does that or how he or she can do it for the customer. Once again, the broader capabilities of vendor company are on the table.

Even intangibles can fill a customer's needs. Consider a new buyer of complicated products or services. The salesperson's ability to relate past success stories about smoothly run installations and operations may be just what an uncertain customer needs. The salesperson is selling reassurance by citing specific related experiences.

Finally, part of the package is the salesperson. The old adage about people buying the salesperson is true. Customers see an effective salesperson and sales process which yield the best possible solution as a benefit. Salespeople can provide access to expertise, industry gossip and networking contacts. The salesperson is the initial interface to the vendor organization; he or she can get things done, especially when other channels don't work.

The Total Package To Address A Wider Set of Needs

So what does a master salesperson bring? Here's what's in the attaché case:

o The features and benefits of the vendor's products or services

o Potential variations on how to do the deal, including payment terms, delivery, installation, support, credit o Customization of the product or service for a specific customer's application

o Past success stories and application ideas proven in other customer situations

o Advice, insights and information that can impact and help formulate future business plans

o Access to expertise of all types both inside and outside the vendor company in the salesperson's personal network

o The salesperson's personal ability to solve problems, get things done for the customer in the vendor organization and, ultimately, to be an ally at the planning table

It All Boils Down To Value

From this list of capabilities, it becomes clear that the salesperson is much more than a describer of products. Whether customers are sophisticated or naive, the salesperson is the expert with a unique perspective, the catalyst who strives to see the whole problem and suggests how to get the problem solved, either directly with the customer or by orchestrating a problem solving process with other people.

Because the salesperson helps uncover, interpret, and reshape the customer's problem, supplying an optimal solution, the salesperson adds value.

A master salesperson does something the customer can't or couldn't do alone. They see what the customer doesn't, they bring a perspectives, special knowledge and alternatives the customer doesn't see.

When the customer experiences this kind of selling, they see and feel value. The customer can buy with confidence not only in the product or service, but in the way it was sold.

Bottom line: the customer gets more, relationships are cemented, competition is held at bay.

Section 2: Getting To The Heart of Selling

Five Fundamental Ideas

After observing and working with master salespeople for many years and selling my own company's consulting services for over 25 years, I believe that there are five ideas about how to find and solve customer needs at the root of every sales transaction. If every salesperson focused on and understood these ideas, they would see themselves as problem solvers, their central and critical role in the sales process. All the techniques, catch-phrases and face-to-face questioning methods typically taught in training classes can augment and help implement this fundamental problem solving role. The key here and now is to learn the concepts. They are not difficult to understand. Mastering them takes practice and coaching.

The five fundamental ideas which ground the salesperson as problem solver are:

1. Find out about the customer and about all the customer's problems.

2. Add value, make a difference.

3. Give the customer options.

4. Make it work.

5. Stay in touch.

1. Find Out About The Customer and All The Customer's Situation

Although it's obvious that asking questions is one of the salesperson's most potent tools, many salespeople, even veterans, don't ask enough of the right questions. Most ask too many of the wrong questions.

Remember, the premise is that if a salesperson can find a broad array of customer needs, then he or she can offer a solution which addresses many of them. That takes asking the right questions in the right way.

Now here is a subtle point. It's common for inexperienced salespeople to ask many questions that gather a lot of information, but don't really contribute to solving the customer's broad array of problems. The results are pages of notes which capture facts but not the needs that could have been surfaced.

Why?

For one thing, most new salespeople are told to ask a lot of questions, and they do. But, the process is not pleasant to watch or experience: the questions are often random, and the customer usually winds up feeling like they have been interrogated.

Probably more important, the reason for asking questions may not be totally clear to the salesperson. After all, the salesperson is looking for the customer to tell him or her what the the need is so he or she can describe the product or service.

What's the big deal?

Consider what kinds of questions a salesperson would ask is he or she had an expanded view of what their role was, what they could do for the customer. That would change the whole questioning strategy. If the salesperson had a better handle on the extended and total package of benefits—all the capabilities of the vendor organization available to the customer—they would ask more focused questions and surface needs they can do something about.

Because of their perspective, master salespeople can recognize patterns of needs in customer and ask penetrating questions which get the customer to see needs they might not have been aware of.

Master salespeople are not shy about probing how a customer feels about a business need, capturing and noting whatever emotional energy the customer has packed into a business problem. If a customer is not confident, uncertain or vague about how to proceed, a master salesperson can tag those personal needs as critical to solve in the solution.

When a salesperson uncovers and understands a customer's business and personal, current and future needs, he or she is better prepared to address them comprehensively.

2. Add Value, Make a Difference

Can you imagine customers cheering a salesperson when he or she enters a conference room? It has happened. Customers are so taken by what the salesperson can do in the problem-solving, catalyst role that they feel grateful.

Customers feel grateful for a salesperson? How?

Adding value is what happens during and after the sales process. Adding value is what salespeople do when they are addressing wide array of customer problems with their extended product notion. A salesperson who adds value can make a difference to how the sales process works, how solutions impact a customer's business, how people feel about the solution, all the while cementing relationships and holding off competition. Salespeople who make a difference—

o Provide continuity from past issues and problems, past purchases and applications to future strategies and customer intentions

o Consider a customer's strategy and long term needs when developing solutions

o Build alliances and loyalty within the company by accommodating the needs of a wide group of stakeholders

o Bring in expertise—technocrats, senior managers or other resources—to offer what value is appropriate for the sake of the customer's business, not just for a sale

o Knows the customer's company—how the business works and what its operating policies are, its culture, the quality of its people o Build a reputation that he or she is dependable, solid and on the company's side, an advocate

I think every salesperson's goal is to be welcomed eagerly by customers in their anticipation of the ideas and insights he or she will have for their problems.

The image comes to mind of a group of customers watching their favorite salesperson from a conference room overlooking visitor's parking. The salesperson emerges from a car and starts walking to the entry. One customer turns to another and says, "At least, now we'll get somewhere."

Now that's adding value.

3. Give The Customer Options

Once a salesperson understands a customer's business and needs, he or she is able to recommend a solution. Most customers are wary of one-solution answers to their problems. They want to see alternatives. They want to be educated about what differentiates the choices a salesperson brings from those of the competition. Customers want to gauge the impact of different solutions on their problem.

When customers gets involved with choosing alternatives, they are literally looking into the future and testing what might be the result. It could involve a demonstration, a test drive, a try-on, a pilot program, a working prototype, or just a rich description of what'll be. The point is, whether he or she is selling suits or communication satellites, the salesperson needs to guide this trying-on process, emphasizing the impact of the features and benefits of different alternatives on customer needs, and helping the customer weigh the good and the bad.

As a result, salespeople have made the buying decision a choice among different options for the customer. The customer makes an informed decision; the salesperson makes a difference to the customer's buying process.

4. Make It Work

The sale is arguably most vulnerable after the customer says "Yes".

A customer-sensitive and highly efficient implementation of a customer's chosen solution is incredibly critical. This is where the customer can renege, cancel, return the goods, continue looking at other vendors and worry about the price.

Unfortunately, many salespeople don't view the immediate after-sale period as part of the sales process, and the idea of making the solution work is often overlooked.

Responsibility for installation, implementation, ramp-up, training or whatever, is handed off to another function. Technical people step in, project managers, customer service representatives, sales assistants, other professionals who will do the work are introduced to the customer. The salesperson, whether he or she is a senior partner or a telephone representative, too often see themselves as off the hook.

If the salesperson has done everything right and built value, this hand-off can make a customer uncomfortable, upset and uncertain. Their guide and counselor is gone, and, in the customer's eyes, they are left to deal with strangers who have no clue about what they bought and why they bought it.

A master salesperson knows this is a dangerous time. He or she will ensure that the products or service and other parts of the whole solution are being spec'ed, built, delivered and installed as promised by people who are knowledgeable about the products, obviously, but, more important, who are also completely briefed on the company and its rationale for buying.

Once more, the salesperson can add value by heading off problems, redirecting his or her own implementation team, giving the customer advice and shouldering the responsibility of fighting the customer's battles internally.

This takes work. It means taking the pulse of different people in the customer company, other buyers, especially those who were skeptical about the solution choice. It means being able to influence internal resources. It also means the salesperson has to be there to ensure the product or service is working as promised and that customers see the benefits that were pledged earlier. The salesperson has to manage expectations and "Buyer's

Remorse", the inevitable let down customers feel after making a choice.

The master salesperson takes this personally. He or she is not off the hook, in fact, most consider themselves on the hook, on top of the post-sale time frame, reselling benefits, ensuring clarity all around and making things happen so that promises made are promises kept.

5. Stay In Touch

Once a relationship has been formed, it must go somewhere. The salesperson can be the guide. How can a salesperson do that? How can a salesperson spend time relationship building with old customers when they are under pressure to produce more revenue from new prospects?

The tendency of many sales people is to overlook an established customer's need for contact, direction and more ideas. In fact, many customers will end a relationship with a vendor because ideas stop flowing. When customers feel they are just being "serviced" by sales people, the relationship built around problem solving and special knowledge of customer problems and needs seems to be diminished. There is a let-down after the sale because the problem-solver turns into an administrator.

This happens all too soon. There is a tendency for the customer to look for more from their vendor just when the primary salesperson is putting the relationship on autopilot.

So, staying in touch is an overlooked idea. Monitoring customer satisfaction, continuing to add value on an ongoing basis and building a long range plan, however informal, for the customer feeds the relationship. Master salespeople have a direction for each customer in mind. Now that they are aware of the customer's business strategy, needs and future plans, they should be able to craft something of a product and service migration strategy, at least in their own minds.

To implement that strategy, salespeople need to make additional sales calls which have value and bring fresh ideas to the customer. Now that a relationship based on value has been established, the salesperson's role is to be a consultant, validating customer needs, sounding out different customer's views of those needs and building support for recommended solutions.

The tendency here is to become complacent. Even experienced salespeople fall into the trap of "stopping by for the order" or just to check in and say hello. In these competitive times, a good sales professional will plan each call, figuring out how to leave a sense a value behind. Some salespeople will provide useful ideas to educate customers about industry developments or stimulate a customer's interest in new ways of doing things. Others will perform a service for the customer, such as collecting and analyzing product usage information. The idea is that in order to continue to get business, the salesperson has to continue to add useful value to the relationship.

Staying in touch takes many forms—from phone calls, to notes and letters with clippings to catch a customer's interest attached, to formal sales calls, invitations to vendor events such as user meetings and informal get togethers outside the office. Whatever the form of the interaction, customers should get something useful to keep the sense of value from the salesperson alive and fresh.

In the corporate world, some master salespeople schedule a formal account review once or twice a year with important accounts. Over several hours, the salesperson and a senior manager from the vendor company with appropriate technical experts meet with the customer and other stakeholders. The customer reports progress with using the product or service and the benefits derived; the sales team acknowledges their vendor efforts to make the product or service effective, and each team recognizes success in a mutually beneficial relationship. Problems are aired and solved, improvement ideas are exchanged, new developments are previewed and plans are made for continuing the relationship, and then everyone goes to a suitable celebratory dinner.

Even excellent corporate salespeople send their "A" list, their very best customers personal notes about new lines or products of potential interest. Financial planners, real estate agents, accountants, insurance people, stockbrokers, and lawyers create newsletters that check-in with the customer base with new information, interesting ideas to save money, expand the business, or whatever. The principle is to stay in touch with value-laden ideas no matter how physically remote from the customer the salesperson is.

Five Ideas At Work

Assembled together, these five ideas portray the role of the master salesperson as an interested and involved member of the customer team. They describe an attitude about the salesperson-customer relationship. The salesperson is not a transactor, even if the sales situation looks like a transaction. The person who buys a pair of socks and learns in the process about how to care for them from the salesperson will think about that added value when the next opportunity for buying socks comes around. The new mutual funds customer who invests over the phone and who is reassured by the telephone representative that the purchase will show up in the customer's account the next day, explaining how to check electronically, hangs up with a positive impression about the whole buying process.

Instead of transactions, the master salesperson creates a relationship, one in which the salesperson invests time to learn about, reflect on and develop ideas for the customer. Regardless of whether it is a brief added comment or an extended sales process involving a sales team, the impact on the customer is the same.

The ultimate outcome is a sense of added value and trust. Master salespeople who have really done it right can find themselves invited back again and again to the customer's planning table. It's that sense of making a meaningful contribution which keeps many salespeople going. Beyond the commissions and the leased cars, aside from the recognition awards and golf meetings, the salesperson finds being a valued partner at the heart of selling.

Section 3: Skills at the Heart of Selling

The reminder of this guide outlines skills for implementing the five fundamental selling ideas. Here's how to use it:

1) Review the outline.

2) Check which skills you are doing now and should be doing more frequently.

3) Isolate those skills you are not doing now.

4) Pick no more than two to work on for a week. But, just do it. For more advice on how to be successful in improving those skills, see Section 4.

5) Enlist your sales manager or other salespeople for advice or role play practice.

6) Expect the best and aim for improvement.

Find Out About The Customer and The Customer's Situation

1. Ask logical, in-depth probing questions to better understand the customer's situation

What To Do	How To Do It
Get the Big Picture.	• Find out what the customer's situation is, what's on their plate, what the challenges ahead are, note the facts and how different people in the customer company feel and what they are expected to make happen. • Ask about problems the customer is experiencing, why those problems came about.
Probe the needs in a logical way with open ended questions	• Ask how customers feel about where the business is now and where it is headed. • Ask customers to speculate on how challenges or needs developed. • Ask customers to evaluate how well attempts to resolve the business issue in the past have worked. • Ask customers what their buying criteria are and their expectations are for a successful resolution to the challenges they've identified.

Trace the impact.	• Ask questions about how problems impact different parts of the customer's business in terms of increased cost, lost efficiency and waste, poor quality, low morale, etc.
	• Find out what is at stake for each customer, personally, in the current situation.
Measure the pain.	• Work with the customer to quantify, in terms of cost, man-hours or quality measures how different functions are influenced by problems.
Sort out different views held by people in the customer company.	• Identify what is at stake for each functional area, each affected stakeholder in the company.
Find out the stakeholders' and customer's biases.	• Ask different people what they think the problem is and what the solution to the problems should look like. Get their preferences out on the table and consider where they're coming from—what they would buy— when you make recommendations.
	• Find how customers personally view the business and the challenges they're facing.
Ask more open-ended questions than close-ended questions.	• Get the customer talking about the needs instead of asking questions answered by yes or no; ask why and how, what if questions.

Find Out About The Customer and The Customer's Situation

2. Focus closely on what the customer says and how he/she says it

What To Do	How To Do It
Repeat.	• Restate what you think the customer said without bias, evaluation or interpretation; ask the customer if what you said was an accurate reflection of what the customer said.
Track.	• Show the customer you're tracking his/her thoughts by using body language such as leaning forward, nodding agreement, and saying "uh-huh" as you listen and take notes.
Follow digressions.	• Ask the customer to expand points and, after discussing the answers, guide the customer back to the major themes you were discussing.
Pull thoughts together and confirm.	• Show the customer you have listened by summarizing the customer's needs in a confirming single statement and in an appropriate post-call communication.
Pay attention to body language.	• Leaning back means withdrawl or disapproval, fidgeting, watching the clock, sounding suddenly dimissive or hurried are all red flags. • Become sensitive to reactions to questions.

Find Out About The Customer and The Customer's Situation

3. Recognize what the customer wants from the buying process and he/she wants to be sold

What To Do	How To Do It
Work with the customer on working defining your working relationship.	• Ask the customer to think about recent experiences with sales people and to tell you what was effective and what was not effective about the selling process. • Ask the customer what role you, the salesperson, are expected to play in the sales process. • Remain flexible and be willing to modify the sales process when it makes sense or when it helps the customer out • Describe how your sales process works and ask the customer for agreement or modify the process to meet the customer's needs. • Generate different ideas with the customer on the most appropriate ways to introduce your company, its products and services to the customer's company. • Offer the customer choices on how to move the sales process forward at each step.

Find Out About The Customer and The Customer's Situation

4. Ask questions that reflect knowledge of how things get done in the customer's business

What To Do	How To Do It
Use your experience to probe the customer's problem.	• Ask the customer if he or she has considered the impact of business needs on areas which you know are easily and predictably overlooked. • Ask the customer to change perspective and look at his or her needs from a different point of view, say, as a customer of the business or as a vendor. • Suggest sources or causes of problems which may be evident to you but not to the customer. • Discuss how other companies you know have experienced the same or related problems.
Take a closer look when the situation warrants it.	• Propose a focused effort for you to study the customer's business need in greater depth. • Call in resources from your personal and business network who can clarify, help uncover issues and address the customer's needs.
Use your familiarity with the business to probe how the customer describes the problems they are experiencing	• Ask questions that start with "How do you determine, calculate, evaluate...?" • Focus on areas you know are problematic in other companies.

Find Out About The Customer and The Customer's Situation

5. Confirm how customer's needs impact his/her goals and concerns

What To Do	How To Do It
Ask probing questions.	• For each perceived need, drill down into the details, finding out how the need evolved, what has been done, what has changed, how people feel about the problem
Determine how serious the need is.	• Quantify, if possible, the impact of the need. • Surface costs of delay, errors, inefficiencies, lack of consistency or reliability, opportunities lost, and organizational problems. • Get the customer to state what should happen that isn't or what is happening that shouldn't and what that means.
Summarize by stating the implications of the need.	• Make connections to implications the customer might not see. • Draw conclusions about what the total impact of the need might be on the organization.
Ask the customer if he/she agrees.	• Ask how the customer feels about the needs and implications. • Ask the customer why he/she feels it would be important to address the need, how addressing the need would help. • Probe what the customer sees happening in the future if nothing was done.

Find Out About The Customer and The Customer's Situation

6. Know enough about the customer's business to the significance and prevalence of his/her needs

What To Do	How To Do It
Study the market segment.	• Learn how the market segment works, what recent history has been, current practices and trends, problems in achieving goals, typical solutions to problems. • Identify who the big players in the market segment are and what makes them distinctive. • Be clear about what the economic drivers of the segment are, how money is made, what different business models are in use. • Get a sense of what your customer's customers think.
Demonstrate your understanding.	• Ask questions about industry or segment issues using jargon and terms that reflect your familiarity with concepts. • Bring up topics that other companies or representatives of the segment are known to be dealing with as well as current events (industry or segment news and regulatory changes).
Become part of the customer's world.	• Subscribe to and write for industry or segment magazines and journals. • Speak at local and regional gatherings, become a member of advisory groups or associations, attend conferences and

	conventions.
Make links between the customer's needs and what you see or know about from different industries or segments.	• Show your understanding of the customer's situation, problems or issues by relating stories about how other industries or segments have addressed similar challenges. • Emphasize how the customer's situation may be unique, despite the similarities to other companies.

Add Value, Make A Difference

7. Offer the customer insights, ideas and alternatives that make sense to him/her

What To Do	How To Do It
Show the customer how much you understand about their business, the situation and what others are doing.	• State your opinion and take a position on issues relevant to the customer. • Relate what other customers are doing, if appropriate. • Offer creative solutions to problems; don't edit your imagination.
Take an active role in helping.	• Suggest a variety of resources other than your company which may be helpful in solving the customer's problems whether the problems are the ones you are specifically seeing them about or others they mention. • Help build new and emerging ideas about the customer's business through your involvement in planning sessions with at the customer's company. • Act as a sounding board and "teacher" on a wide variety of issues whenever possible.

Add Value, Make A Difference

8. Reassure the customer that the sales team has experience in addressing similar needs

What To Do	How To Do It
Tell the customer success stories.	• Find out the specific impact of your product/service has had on former or existing customers. Tell the customer stories about how others have succeeded with your product or service as well as other values your organization offers.
Empathize.	• Show the customer you know what keeps him or her awake at night. • Tell stories about how other customers felt about similar problems.
Show the customer you know the market segment.	• Attend and make presentations at trade or professional organizations and associations. • Give the customer articles from business trade or professional publications that both inform the customer and show him or her you understand the issues facing the marketplace and the advantages and disadvantages of different approaches.
Share your experience.	• Tell the customer how to get the best use from your product or service, based on what others customers have done.

Give a verbal resume of your colleagues.	• The customer has to know who else is involved from your company. If you're on your own, let the customer know about the people in your network. Show the customer your bench strength and the experience of your colleagues.

Add Value, Make A Difference

9. Find additional valuable resources that might help address customer needs

What To Do	How To Do It
Connect the customer with your network.	• Identify a network of useful resources the customer could call on. Link the customer to other customers and resources who have similar interests and needs or can help.
Go beyond the obvious.	• Pay attention to the customer's other business needs in addition to those your product or service is designed to address.
Bring in other experts.	• Be the link between your customer and others; act as a referrer and introducer, play a role in helping the customer solve a need unrelated to your product or service.
Search your network for potential helpers.	• Bring your customer's needs—as appropriate—to your personal network. Ask for ideas, "do you happen to know?", etc. • Enlist network members to offer advice or visit your customer with you.
Educate your customer on the "bigger" needs, how others have addressed them.	• Send your customer links, articles, blogs, or other information that might prove insightful. • Show you're involved with helping the customer pursue answers to bigger problems.

Add Value, Make A Difference

10. Look beyond the immediate reason for calling on the customer to consider related important needs.

What To Do	How To Do It
Plan with the customer.	• Ask the customer about the future and help test ideas; tell the customer what needs you think will eventually emerge in time.
Educate the customer.	• Bring your knowledge of market segment direction and trends up to date. Offer the customer information that may not be directly related to your product/service. • Describe how to optimize your solution by pointing out the impact of the product or service on related needs. • Ask questions about the larger business issues that concern the customer.
Look for a wider set of needs than product/service needs.	• Probe for needs in training, implementation, delivery, credit, customization or tailoring, after-sale support, monitoring effectiveness, etc. • Probe for sales process needs like helping document the customer's problem, assessing how stakeholders perceive the need, calling on decision makers, conducting demos to increase interest and certainty of the solutions.

Add Value, Make A Difference

11. Always remain frank and straightforward in telling the customer and others in the client company what you see

What To Do	How To Do It
Be physically "present" when dealing with the customer.	• Maintain eye contact. • Answer directly, even if the answer is painful for you and the customer. • Listen actively and effectively. • Take notes and ask pertinent probes. • Monitor your own attention; stay focused on what the customer is saying.
Deal directly with account-related problems when they arise.	• Address problems as soon as you are aware of them. • Maintain an even emotional tone. • Offer your interpretation of the account-related problem and suggest a solution. • Ask the customer for his/her ideas for solutions. • Admit when you or your organization are wrong or may not offer the best solution. • Think of ways to "make it up" to the customer if a problem has gotten out of hand.

Show your willingness to bring up sensitive or uncomfortable topics.	• If you see, hear or notice something the customer should know about, mention it. • Be diplomatic about addressing sensitive issues, choose words carefully, especially when telling the customer something he/she will find difficult to listen to. • Use a sincere and respectful tone of voice when describing touchy topics.
Follow through on promises, tasks, communications and anything else you commit to.	• Review your commitments before ending a meeting or a call. • Under promise, over deliver. • Ask the customer what his/her expectations were for delivery or completion of the next step of the sales process. • Keep the customer informed about the status of progress.

Give The Customer Options

12. Tell the customer how your company, its products and services are uniquely different than competitors'

What To Do	How To Do It
Differentiate tangible solutions.	• Clearly show the customer how your product/service's features and benefits compare with competitors' • Tell the customer the advantages and shortcomings of what you offer. • Show respect for your competitors' capabilities and offerings while pointing out differences with yours.
Differentiate the intangibles.	• Explain your company's business philosophy or strategy; make it real by giving the customer an example of what's in it for him or her. • Be clear about the options the customer has in structuring the elements of a deal: terms, credit, availability, delivery, installation, on-going support, as appropriate. • Have war stories ready about how your company ensures satisfaction for its customers. • Describe successful existing and past relationships with other customers. • Identify the expertise your company has and which specific experts the customer will have access to. • Describe how you personally will work with the customer to make the product or service work.

Give The Customer Options

13. Show the customer alternative approaches that address his/her needs in different ways.

What To Do	How To Do It
Present solutions that the customer can successfully use.	• Be sensitive to the customer's level of user sophistication. • Judge the customer's readiness for more advanced solutions and what impact those would have on successful implementation and use, assessing resources, skill levels, availability, other initiatives the customer is engaged in.
Offer choices, clearly defining trade offs and benefits both tangible and intangible.	• Explain how each alternative will address the customer's need, what the relative impact will be and the costs. • Remember to emphasize the intangible benefits of each choice—support, effectiveness of training, ease of use, upgradeability, delivery, etc. • Present a range of solutions from relatively simple to relatively sophisticated to demonstrate possibilities and potential future solutions without being too complex.

Be creative about combining, configuring, or staging in solutions.	• If possible, mix and match elements of the solution, pointing out advantages and disadvantages of non-standard approaches.
	• Be creative about modifying elements of the solution to match the customer's situation.
	• Consider creating or recommending to the customer a "starter kit", layering in progressively more advanced features over time.

Give The Customer Options

14. Provide clear, easy-to-understand examples of how the product or service will help the customer and his/her customers

What To Do	How To Do It
Create a line of sight between your product/service and the customer's customers.	• Illustrate the positive impact of your product or service on not only the customer's business but the customer's customer. • Use stories, data, testimonials to prove your point. Provide referrals.
Refer the customer to others who are using similar application solutions.	• Bring hard data to the customer from other organizations. • Arrange visits or discussions with other customers who are experiencing the full value of the relationship with your company.
Run pilots in the customer's organization.	• As appropriate, establish a trial of your product or service in the customer's organization, providing training and support. • Collect data from the trial and relate to customer needs—cost saving, increased capability, efficiency, quality, etc.
Provide detailed illustrations, demos and simulations of how your product or service would work.	• Create realistic case scenarios, showing projected quantifiable results under different conditions. • Bring the customer to carefully staged demos, illustrating different ways to use your product or service.

Give The Customer Options

15. Clearly link product/service features and benefits to those needs that are important to the customer

What To Do	*How To Do It*
Focus your presentations on customer "hot buttons"	• Show how your product/service features can make a direct impact on what your customer has identified as important issues to him/her. • Restate and confirm what you have learned are the customer's hot buttons.
Connect solution to customer need.	• Understand the impact of a product or service will have on each business need. • For each product or service feature, be ready to describe at least one benefit relevant to the customer. • Use the customer's own words to describe the benefit to the solution, learned from prior probing. • Quantify benefits of your product/service based on your personal experience with the use of the product/service with other customers.

Show the customer it works.	• Demonstrate benefits in a hands-on trial or by visiting current users with the customer.
	• Introduce the customer to customers who are willing to reliably provide testimonials about the impact of your product/service.
	• Show the solution has a direct personal benefit to the customer.
	• Show evidence that your product/service solution will work. For example, perform a comparative before and after study that measures the impact of your product/service with a prior method.
Confirm that the customer gets it.	• Ask those involved with the decision process what advantages they see in using your product/service and the related services your company provides.

Give The Customer Options

16. Creatively and directly address obstacles raised by the customer

What To Do	How To Do It
Pay attention to fully understanding the obstacle.	• Listen to the customer's objection carefully and restate it in your words to confirm your understanding. Be certain whether it is an objection to the sale or a question that simply needs an answer. Don't let an obstacle pass by unaddressed. • Ask several probing questions to get to the root of what the obstacle is.
Educate the customer if he or she is mistaken or misinformed.	• If the customer has misunderstood you or has a misperception, correct him or her by clearly explaining how your product or service works or how the sales process will proceed.
Show data to prove a point to a skeptical customer.	• If the customer is skeptical, present credible evidence backed up by data, if possible, of your product/service's effectiveness. Anecdotes about other customer's experience may also work.
Get the customer to problem solve.	• Ask the customer to define what kind of resolution to conflicts or obstacles are acceptable; tell the customer the feasibility of what he or she is asking for, and, if you can't deliver, develop alternatives.
Weigh the good and the bad.	• If you or your product can't do something the customer wants, tell him or her. But outweigh that disadvantage by reinforcing all the ways the customer's needs are addressed.

Make It Work

17. Take steps to get things done within your company for the customer

What To Do	How To Do It
Know your own players.	• Pinpoint key resources in your company who can personally resolve customer problems.
Prepare the customer.	• Tell the customer how your company works, what kinds of people are lined up to help the customer, what your company's unique operating practices are. Tell the customer what to expect.
Give the customer problem-avoidance advice.	• Let the customer know the best way to avoid different types of typical vendor-customer relationship problems before they occur.
Personally take on the customer's problems.	• Go to bat for the customer; don't transfer the customer's problem to someone inside your company without remaining involved.
Be the customer's advocate.	• Let the customer know you fight for the customer's needs inside your own company.
Demonstrate your political savvy to the customer.	• Show the customer you know how to get things done in your own company; tell the customer you know the priorities and needs of internal functions within your own company, ask people in those functions to specify the best way to work with them.

Make It Work

18. Use experts to determine how the customer can make best use of your company's products or service

What To Do	How To Do It
Bring in the big guns.	• Identify experts or executives in your company and outside network who have something of value to contribute to the customer's business needs—experience and knowledge, access to information, a wider perspective.
Get help.	• Consult with an expert on how the problem should be solved and, if you can, solve the problem with them in front of the customer.
Leave nothing to chance.	• Don't let the expert come in cold; customers don't want automatic answers. Take time to prep the expert for a sales call by explaining the customer's business needs, the application problem and what the customer expects from the expert's visit.
Gather smart people around the customer's table.	• Convene a working session using the experts from your company as well as the customer's company to figure out how to approach bigger problems and implement solutions.

Make It Work

19. Show the customer how the proposed solutions are financially worth the price

What To Do	How To Do It
Review and summarize outcomes.	• Collect results or outcome data from the customer's use of your product or service. Quantify results and compare with projections or expected outcomes. • Collect testimonials from specific users within the customer organization. • If possible, collect reactions and impressions from the customer's customer.
Review the total package of value from your organization.	• Restate the benefits associated with the features of the product or service as well as the intangible benefits of doing business with your company. • Emphasize how responsive your organization has been, the skill and professionalism with which problems had been addressed, how reliable support was delivered and the caring and empathy that was demonstrated by customer service personnel.

Make It Work

20. Build relationships with a number of people in the customer's company

What To Do	How To Do It
Create a support base.	• Call on a broad base of customers at different levels of the customer's organization to get your name and your product/service known through the company.
Understand the pressures on people.	• Probe for the business needs of people at different levels of the customer company.
Put your ear to the ground.	• Listen to what different people in the customer organization expect from the performance of your product/service.
Get their people on-board.	• Trace the beneficial impact of your product/service on different functions in the organization and explain these to the individuals in those functions. • Know your customer's company politics. Be sensitive to the likes and dislikes of different people in the organization who may play a role in a buying decision. • Restate the benefits—the total package of value—the customer's company is receiving from working with your company.

Make It Work

21. Clarify the sales team's ongoing role in the account

What To Do	How To Do It
Be clear about your role and the role of others on the sales team.	• Clearly tell the customer what your role will be in the future. If someone else is going to be the primary customer contact, explain that person's credentials and experience. If you are involved more closely with implementation, explain what you will be doing.
Monitor usage.	• Remain up-to-date on how the customer's company is using your products and services; frequently call on your internal resources to determine the status of the customer's business and how happy the customer is.
Remain in the loop.	• Have your internal resources copy you on all relevant correspondence. • Attend internal meetings; listen carefully for emerging issues and successes.

Make It Work

22. Make sure that others in your company are informed about the customer's needs, business strategy, customer challenges and how he/she wants to do business

What To Do	How To Do It
Communicate to your internal team.	• Develop an "account history" memo and circulate it to different support or service areas within your company, highlighting and updating information that may be relevant to each. Identify key internal personnel who are involved with delivering service and brief them on the account history and personnel. • Develop an organization chart of the customer's company and use that to support your explanation of the account's needs. Tell your people who's changing jobs in the customer's company. Consult your resources about the customer's emerging ideas and plans; gather ideas from them for the customer.
Go beyond the current need to paint of picture of the customer's business situation	• Explain the customer's business context: History, successes, competitors, current situation, reputation, anything that can help the team relate to how the solution will help the customer achieve his/her goals.
Bring your people to the customer's planning table.	• Include different support personnel in meetings to introduce them to customers and to familiarize them with the unique needs of the account.

Stay In Touch

23. Give the customer a good reason to see you on follow-up calls

What To Do	How To Do It
Be specific.	• Announce the purpose of your visit, indicate how you'd like to accomplish that purpose and ask for the customer's agreement. Listen to how narrow or wide the customer wants the discussion to be.
Be precise.	• Present an agenda of items to discuss, get the customer's input and put a time limit on the meeting.
Call ahead.	• Tell the customer your purpose when you make the call. Make requests for information over the phone, if possible. • Know how frequently your customer wants you to check in.
Talk to others.	• Do basic information gathering with a variety of customer personnel rather than taking the decision-maker's time.
Brief your colleagues.	• If calling with others from your company, give them enough information to understand the current account situation, the purpose of the call, on whom you will be calling and their role in the discussion.

Stay In Touch

24. Present post-sale ideas that are unique, insightful, forward-looking and fresh

What To Do	How To Do It
Identify persistent problems.	• Ask questions about business in general and operating concerns in particular that go beyond the scope of your company's product/service.
Ask about the impact of problems.	• Determine how the problems affect the operation of the business.
Make recommendations that will benefit the customer.	• Offer ideas that you know may work, based on your experience and knowledge. • Act as a consultant and make suggestions that your company may or may not have a solution for.
Make referrals.	• Name companies and individuals who can provide expertise in helping the customer learn about different ways of doing business.
Be creative.	• Use your outsider perspective to suggest approaches that might be different and provocative. • Get the customer to brainstorm a number of alternatives. • Ask what-if questions that stimulate thinking.

Stay In Touch

25. Make sure the customer experiences the benefits of the solution you recommended.

What To Do	How To Do It
Watch the customer in action.	• Observe the product/service in use to assure it is being implemented as designed or if modifications are effective. Correct misapplications and procedures.
Ask for opinions and feelings.	• Interview the people who use the product/service. See if they are getting the benefits promised during the sales process.
Offer your opinion.	• Explain how to better use your product or service. Show the customer what others have found. Give us tips and advice.
Educate the customer.	• Invite the customer to meetings and seminars where they will be exposed to new industry trends, products and services.

Stay In Touch

26. Stay current on the customer's business, its strategy, recent changes and emerging needs

What To Do	How To Do It
Call regularly.	• Call on the customer on a regular basis to assure their satisfaction with your product/service and to identify new opportunities.
Call the customer with a purpose, a clear objective.	• Never stop by just to chat; leave the customer with a sense of value—a new idea, a piece of news, something to think about.
Demonstrate interest.	• Follow industry news and events, clip and forward items and information of interest to the customer.
Review how the customers feel about your product or service, and the relationship with your company.	• Conduct a formal account review once or twice a year, assessing the impact and benefits of products or services in use. Show the customer what you can do to upgrade, improve or expand the relationship in the future.
Follow news about the company	• Monitor the customer website, look for news on industry websites, subscribe to RSS feeds and publications.

Stay In Touch

27. Help the customer look into the future and shape new ideas

What To Do	How To Do It
Get the customer to reveal their thoughts and plans.	• Ask the customer to speculate about ideas and plans to expand or modify the business in the future. • Offer advice about how to get there.
Create a plan for the near future.	• Start with a mental plan describing which of your company's offerings you feel the customer's company may grow into over time. • Document and mutually agree in principle on a plan for working together in the future
Look ahead with expert eyes.	• Based on the customer's ideas and plans for the future, project what types of needs the customer may not have anticipated.
Evaluate the customer's Ideas.	• Offer your advice and opinion about the feasibility of the customer's ideas and plans and point out what you feel are potential obstacles and opportunities.
Give the customer your company's agenda for the future.	• Explain the direction your company's product/services will take in the next 2-4 years.
Train the customer.	• Keep the customer up-to-date on how additions and modifications will further optimize the solution.

Section 4: On Improving and Making Progress
What This Guide Can't Do

This guide can't teach you how to increase your enthusiasm level for your product or service. That's really too bad because your personal, sincere enthusiasm and your earnest belief in what you are selling is a bona-fide reason why people buy.

This guide also can't teach you to look at people straight in the eye when you talk to them. That, too, is a differentiator between high and moderately performing salespeople. People like to buy from salespeople who make eye contact. That's not surprising, is it?

Finally, this guide can't teach you how to execute the skills underlying these ideas. The guide is designed to give you the concept; you have to put them to work. You can improve through practice and role plays with peers and managers, or if you're on your own, through tape recorded calls. If that's too much of a hassle, practice by mentally visualizing your call, the questions you want to ask and how you'll feel.

All of these practice suggestions are effective. But there is a lot more to making improvement and progress an integral part of what you do as a salesperson.

What You Can Do

Skill improvement requires a conscious effort to learn and perfect techniques which work. Trying a new skill once or twice in a practice session is a good start, but it's far from achieving proficiency. Here are some suggestions. All of these work together as an improvement system.

1). Recognize the gap between desired and actual.

Often, this is the hardest step. People start improvement when they realize they really need to. They see areas which need work, and they admit it to themselves. Usually, this is a big problem in dealing with veteran salespeople who have sold for so long—and even sold successfully—that they don't see the need to improve. When professional salespeople stop learning, they become vulnerable. Everyone, not matter how proficient and successful, has unproductive habits which need to be broken.

2). Understand that you need to be committed.

Improvement is not a part-time thing. When you see the gap, you have to realize that closing it is not a slam-dunk. There is work to be done, and that means sticking to a plan until there is progress. Unless there is commitment, nothing happens.

3). Have patience; improvement takes time.

The culture tells us to throw things away which don't work. We do the same thing with attempts to improve. If you don't see progress immediately, then the effort is discounted and abandoned. Progress takes time. Improvement comes in steps. If you have a long perspective and get ready for a campaign to reach your goal, you will succeed. Recognize mastery has its own schedule, and it will not be expedited.

4). Measure progress at every opportunity against your starting point.

One tool to use in making improvement is taking measurements of whatever it is you are trying to do. If it's asking questions, record the number of "what-if" questions you ask. If it's making prospecting calls, be rigorous about recording the number per hour or day. If it's products you know, it's the number of features and benefits you can recite. Whatever it is, measure it somehow. Most importantly, use the measures to see how far you've come from the first time you tried it. That's the point. Improvement comes incrementally. Celebrate differences from the starting point.

5). Choose a variety of activities for practice and application.

Doing the same objections handling role play with your manager will only get you so far. Start thinking of alternatives ways to engage in the new skill. Role play with a peer, or just think through problems—anticipate how you would answer hypothetical objections in your mind's eye. Write out your responses in a personal journal. Read books and make notes. Practice presentations in front of a mirror. Give product demonstrations to your family. Don't get stuck on one learning activity.

6). Consolidate what you learn from experience.

The greatest school of all is experience, that is, if you can learn from it. Wise salespeople reflect on each call, each meeting and extract some type of learning conclusion. Instead of dismissing a lost sale to "bad customers" or "tough competition", think through what you could have done differently. These lessons are the most costly to learn, so heed them or else a royal opportunity to improve will pass you by.

7). Practice every day.

People do not emerge from training programs with skill proficiency. At best, they have an understanding of their new skill and a sense of how difficult it will be to actually perform the skill in a work setting. Practice is what it takes to build mastery, lots of practice.

If you decide to work on one skill—like your telephone greeting— work on it every day. Every day. That takes discipline. On the other hand, it's just one thing. If you're also taking measurements, comparing how far you've come, then every day you will see a little bit of progress.

Bottom Line: Follow The Uniqueness

One of the exciting things about the sales profession is that it presents different and often difficult problems to solve with each new opportunity. Master salespeople enjoy newness as well as making links to what they have, in fact, seen before. If you've label yourself as someone who has "seen it all", or you find yourself looking down on customers and their problems because they are too prosaic, take a long walk on the beach or down a country road. You're in the most vulnerable place of your career: you may be guilty of treating customers who present similar characteristics the same exact way.

Master salespeople read people well. What they understand perfectly is that all people like to be treated as individuals. People don't want to feel processed. People don't want to be glad handed or read scripts to, talked to or lectured to. People want to be understood and recognize as unique people.

The salespeople I've worked with over the past decades have demonstrated that if you can genuinely and sincerely attempt to understand a customer's needs—his or her unique circumstance—and present your solution as a fit for those needs, you can be successful. Said another way, if your solution reflects the person, you can win. That solution might have been sold a thousand times before to a thousand different people, but the 1,001 time should be as fresh and insightful to the customer as you can make it.

This is true whether you sell printing services, umbrellas or audits, software, sports equipment or school texts.

Meeting customer needs and helping them buy with confidence is at the heart of selling.

What Works: A Basket of Advice from the Field

One of the truths about sales training which I've come to honor is that we must learn from those who have been down the road before us. Just like the early pioneers, we have to listen to the tales and advice of the people who have crossed the mountain, so to speak. Experience, studied over time, is the best sales trainer.

The advice in this guide is based on the collective experience of the many salespeople I have observed and worked with, researched and interviewed over a 25 year career in sales training.

In later editions of this guide, I plan to incorporate the wisdom and advice of professional salespeople currently working in the field. I would love to hear from you.

Contribute ideas and techniques you've discovered in this guide which you have found effective in practice. Or, offer new ideas and thoughts on master selling which you have discovered. You'll get a credit in our next edition.

Submit your comments to:

Whatworks@c-lensindex.com

www.ingramcontent.com/pod-product-compliance
Lightning Source LLC
Chambersburg PA
CBHW021915190326
41519CB00008B/784